"For all the children who love dogs and art, may your colors bring life to the pages of this book and your imaginations soar as high as the happy tails of these charming furry friends. May each stroke be an adventure and each color a delight! With love and fun, Danny Lima.

Danny Lima
2024

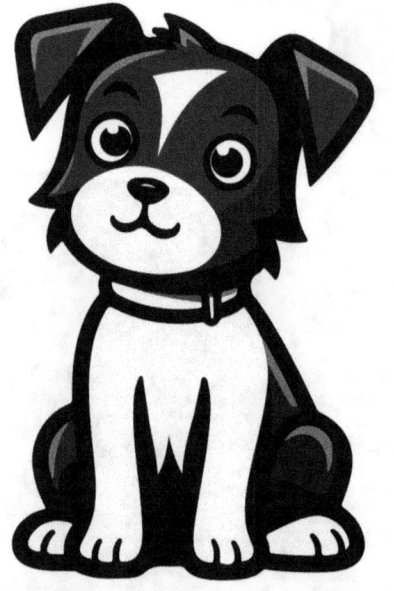
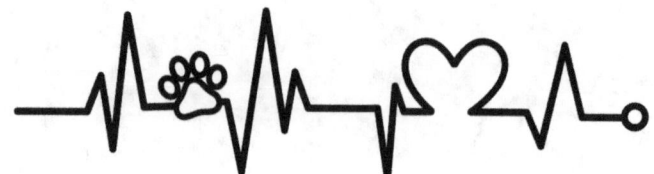

This Book Belongs to:

_____

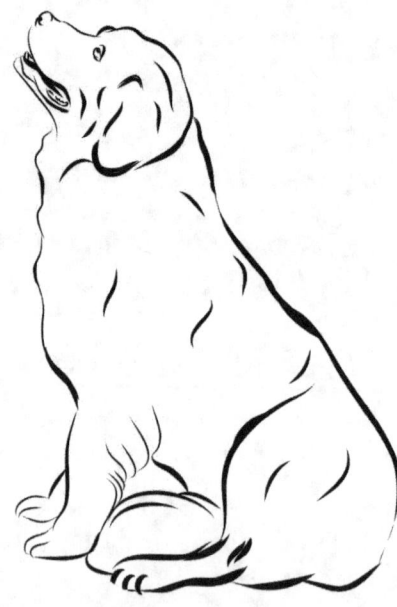

D.L.P.©

Danny Lima publications

ALL RIGHTS RESERVED©
2024

No part of this publication may be reproduced, distributed, or transmitted in any form or by any means, including photocopying, recording, or other electronic or mechanical methods, without the prior written permission of the publisher, except for brief quotations incorporated in critical reviews and other specific noncommercial uses. Any unauthorized replica of this work is prohibited.

D.L. P©

Danny Lima publications

Test Color Page

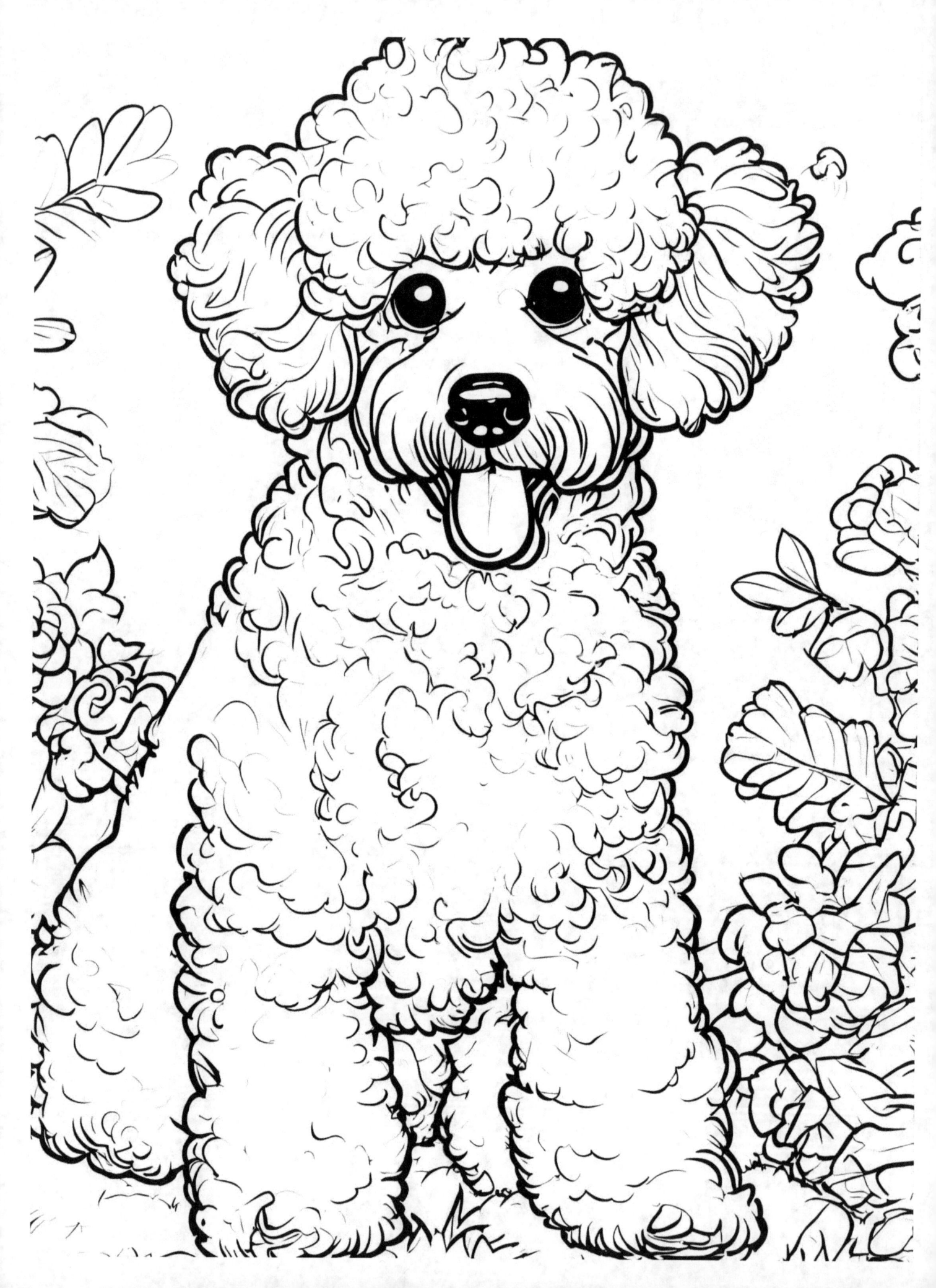

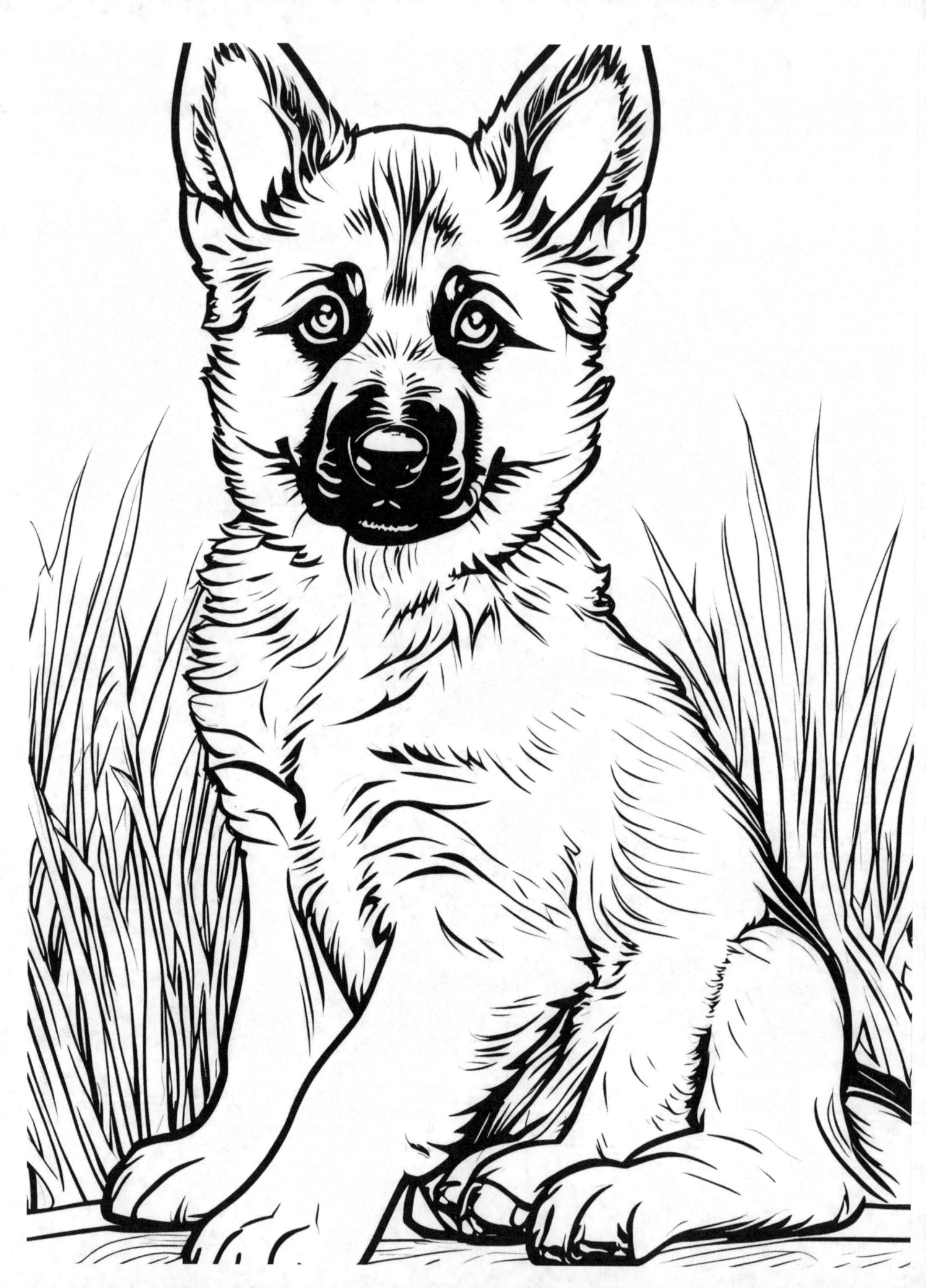

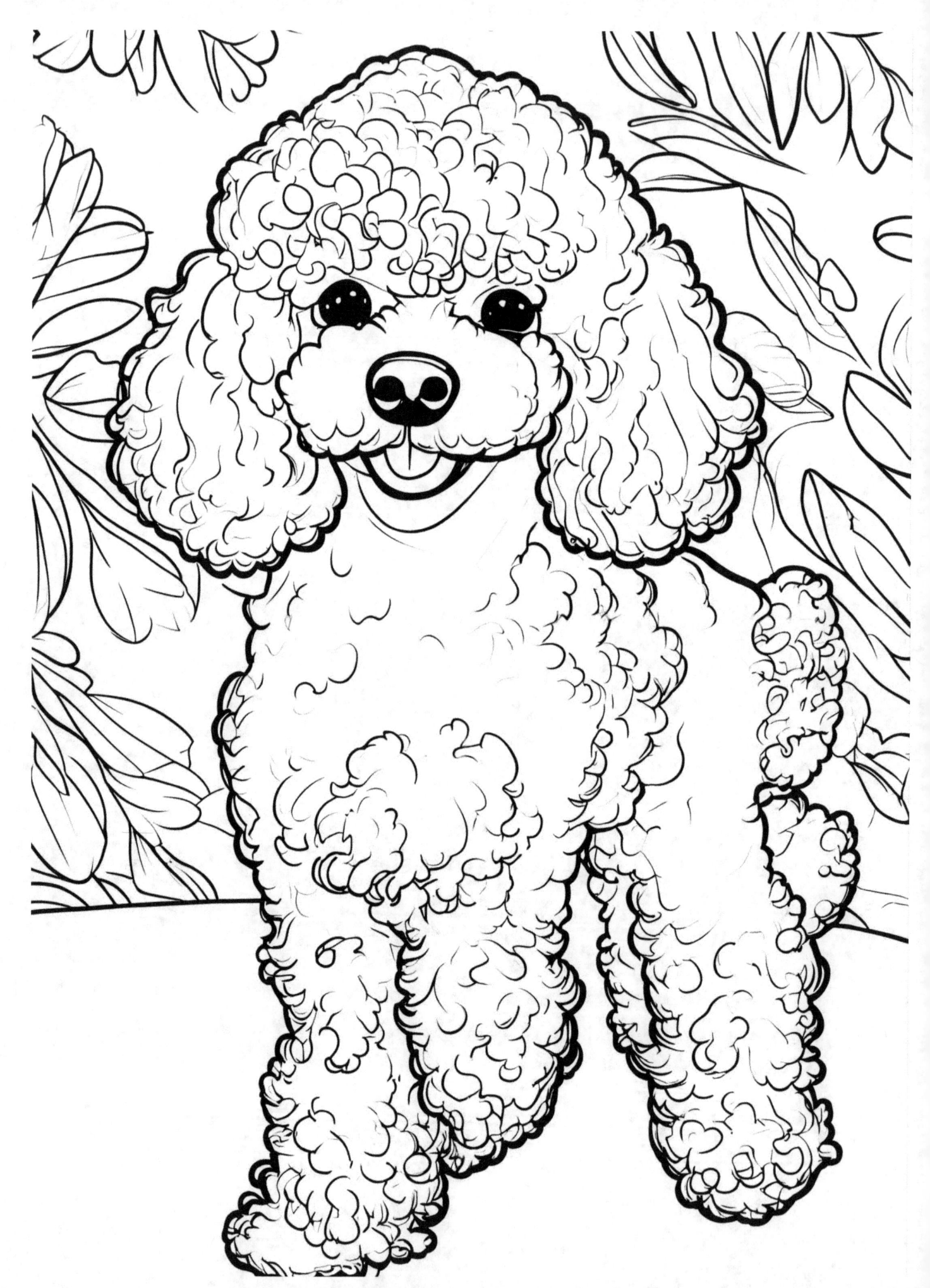

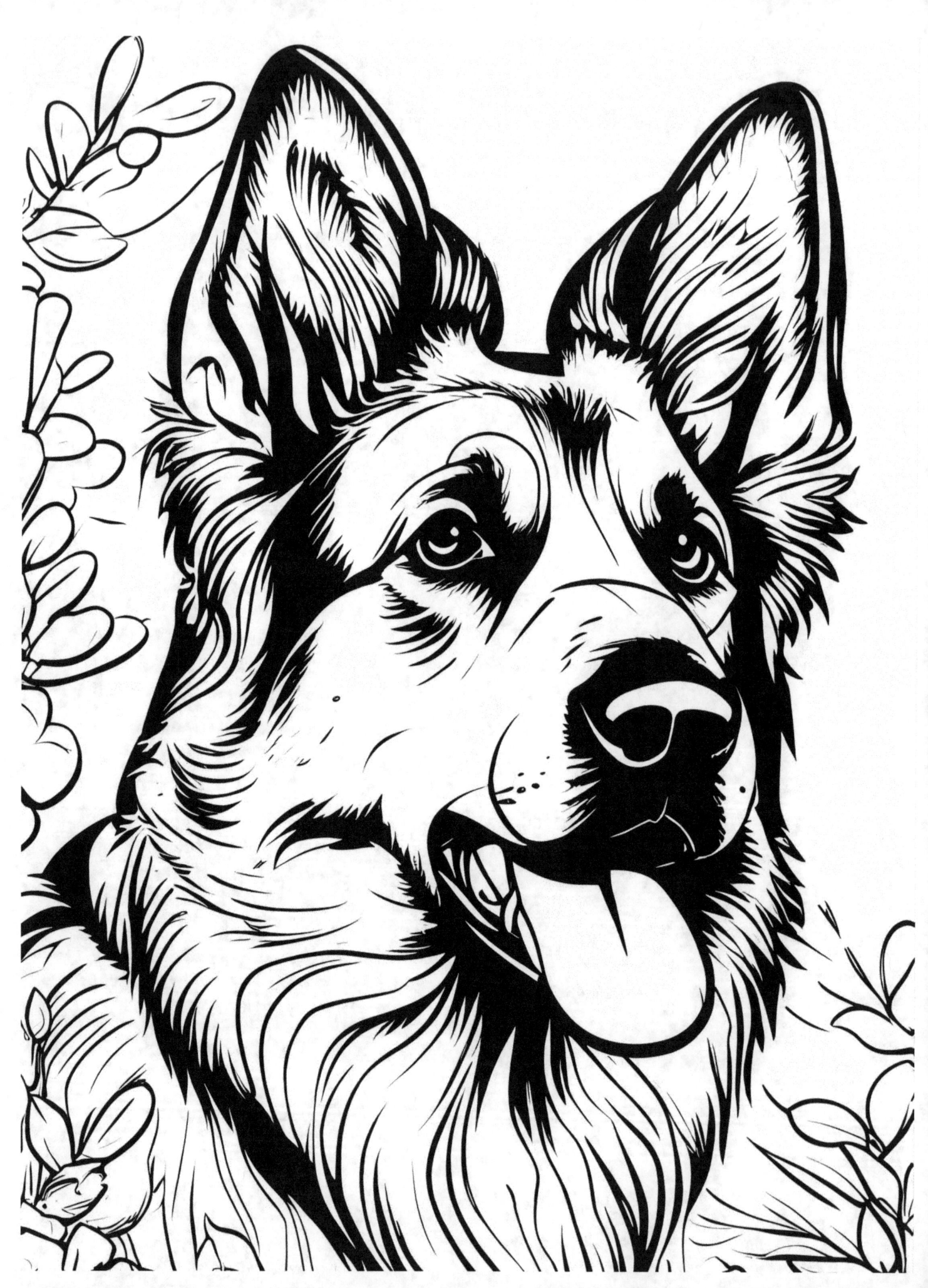

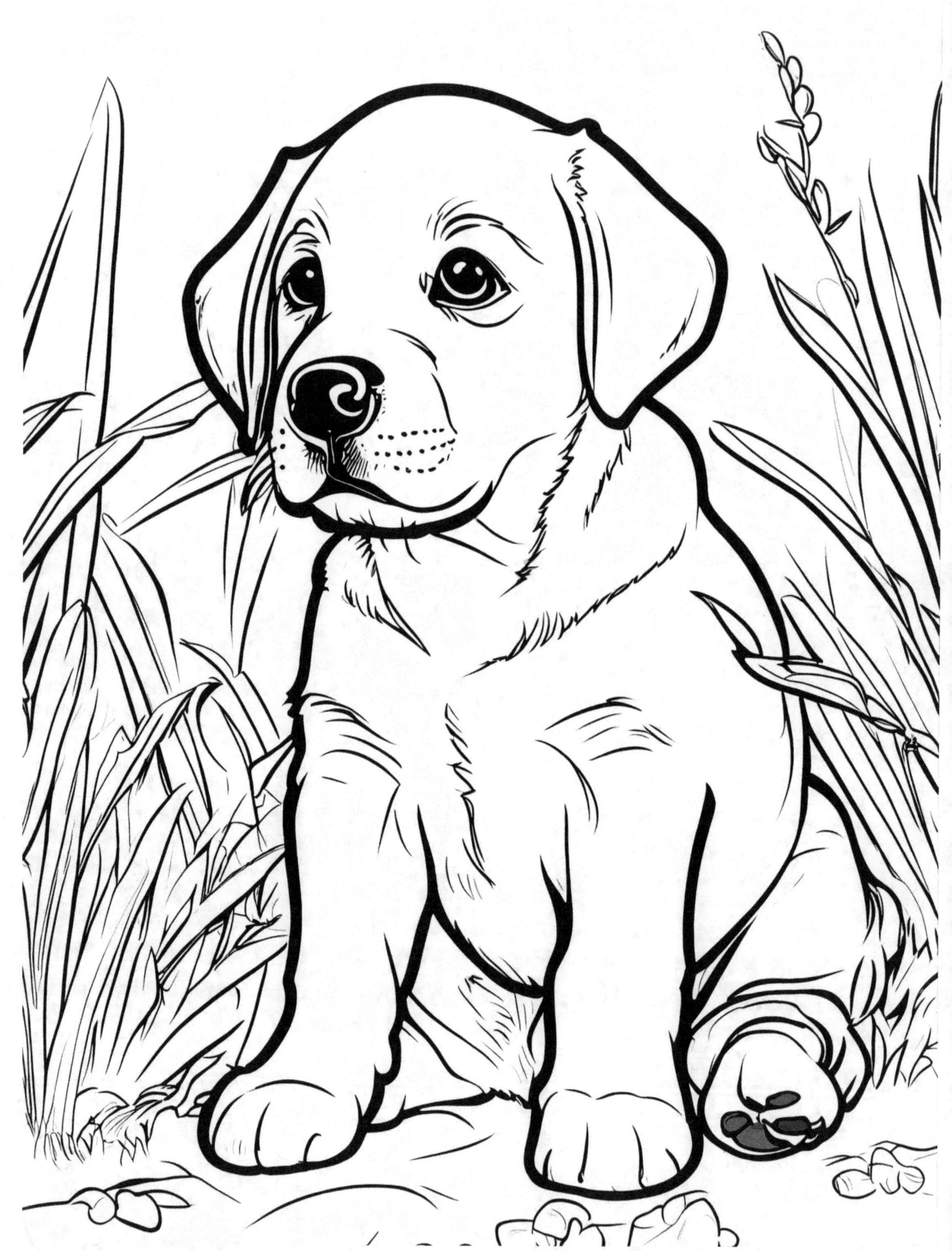

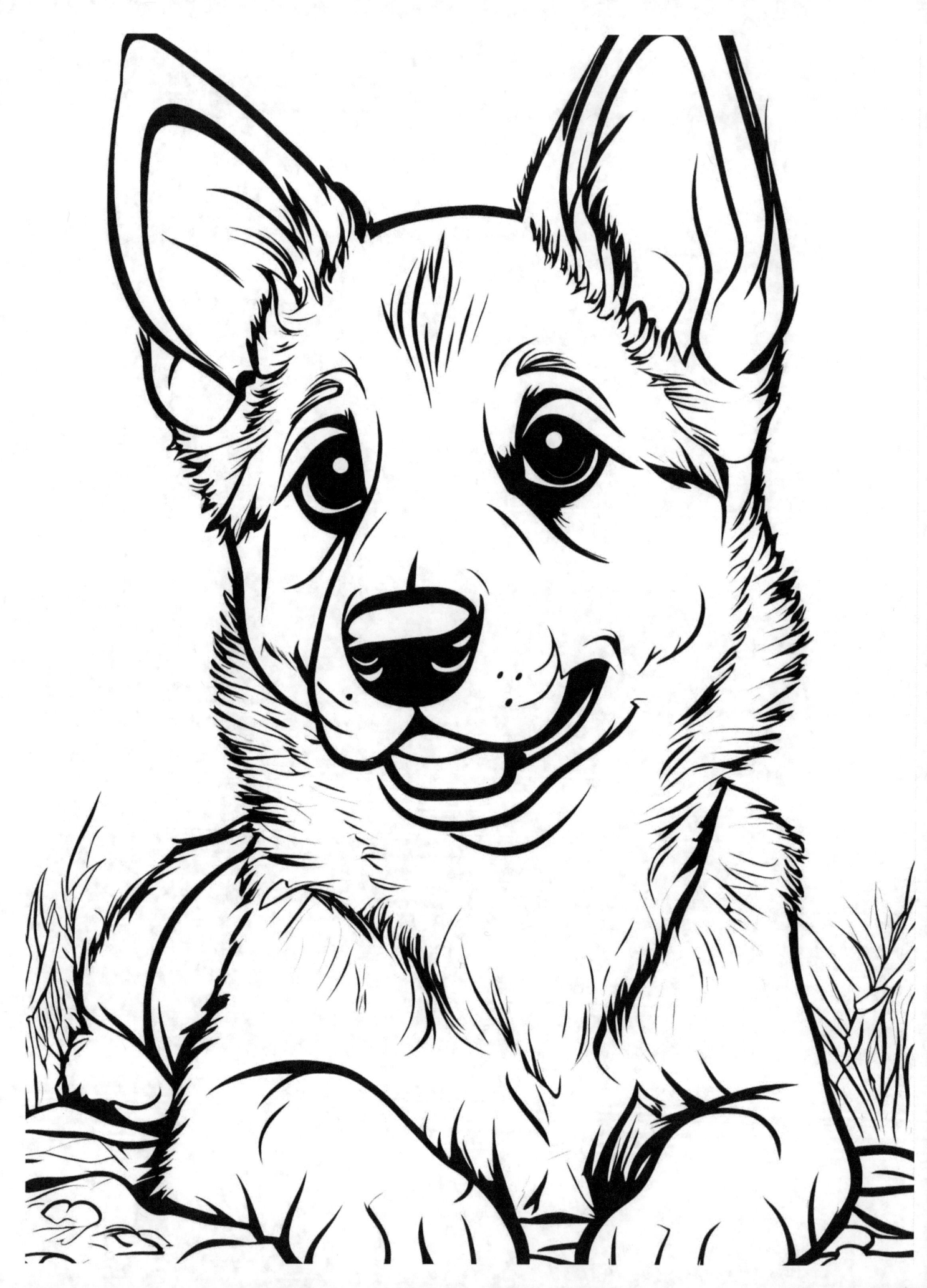

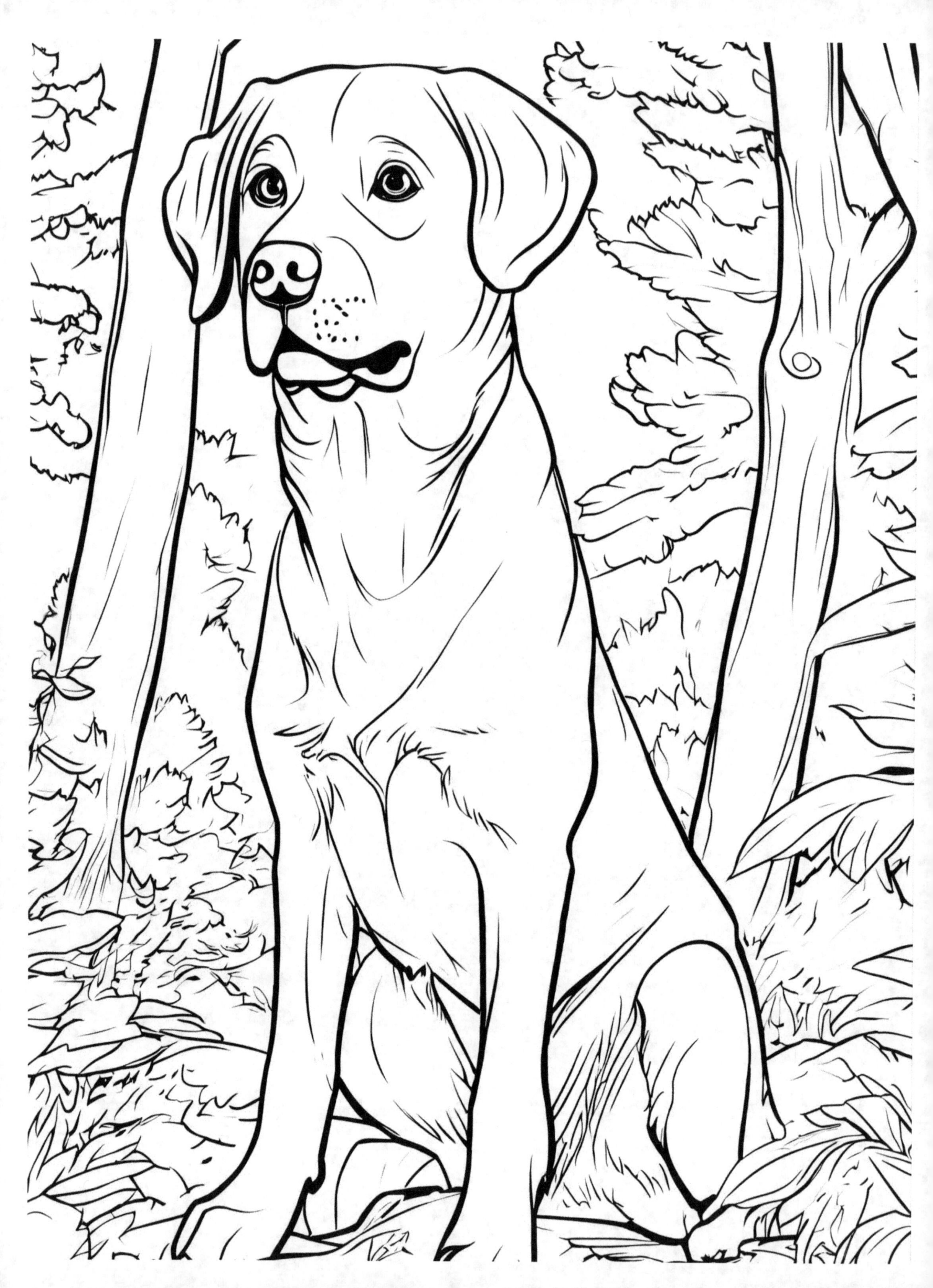

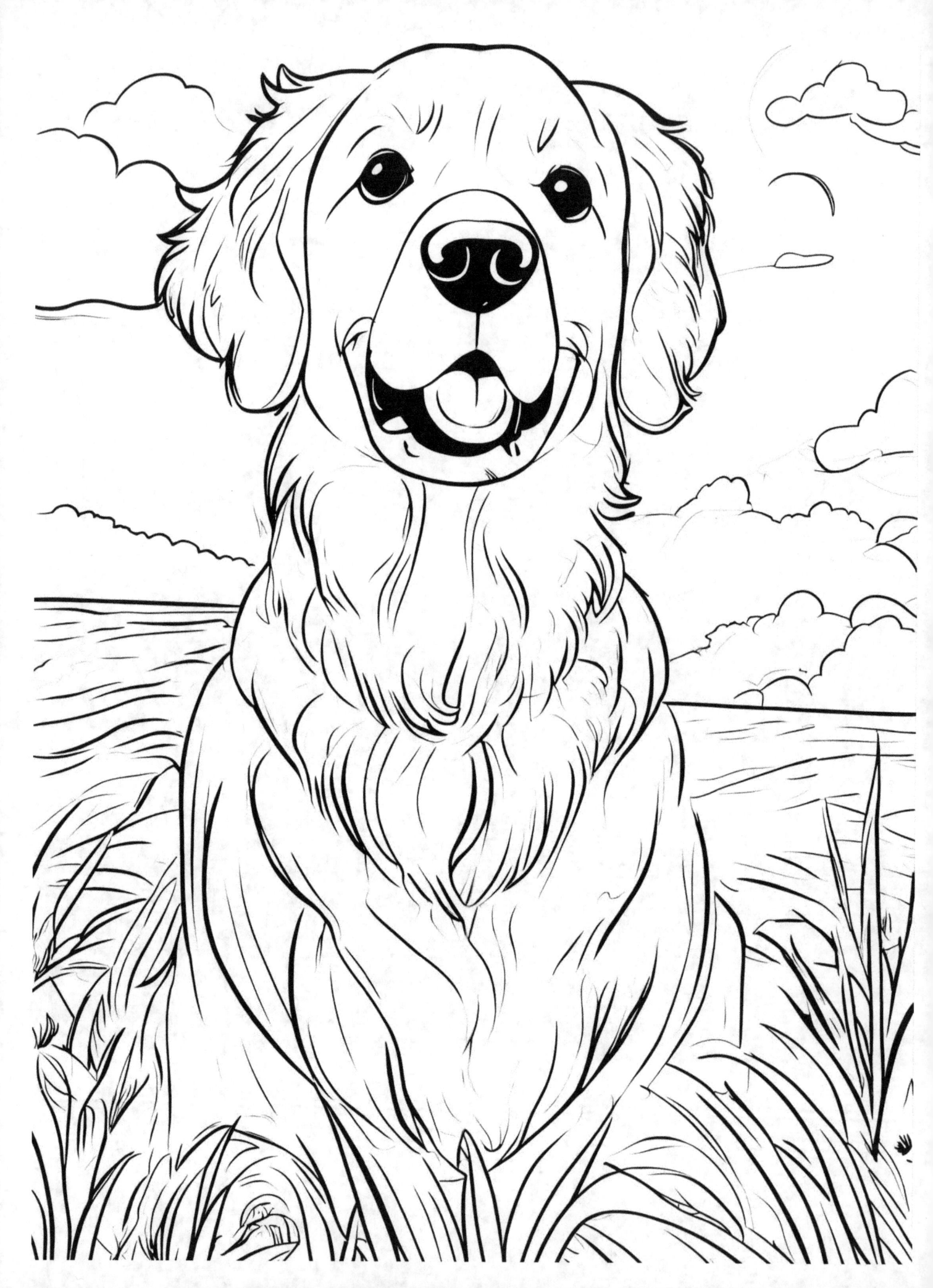

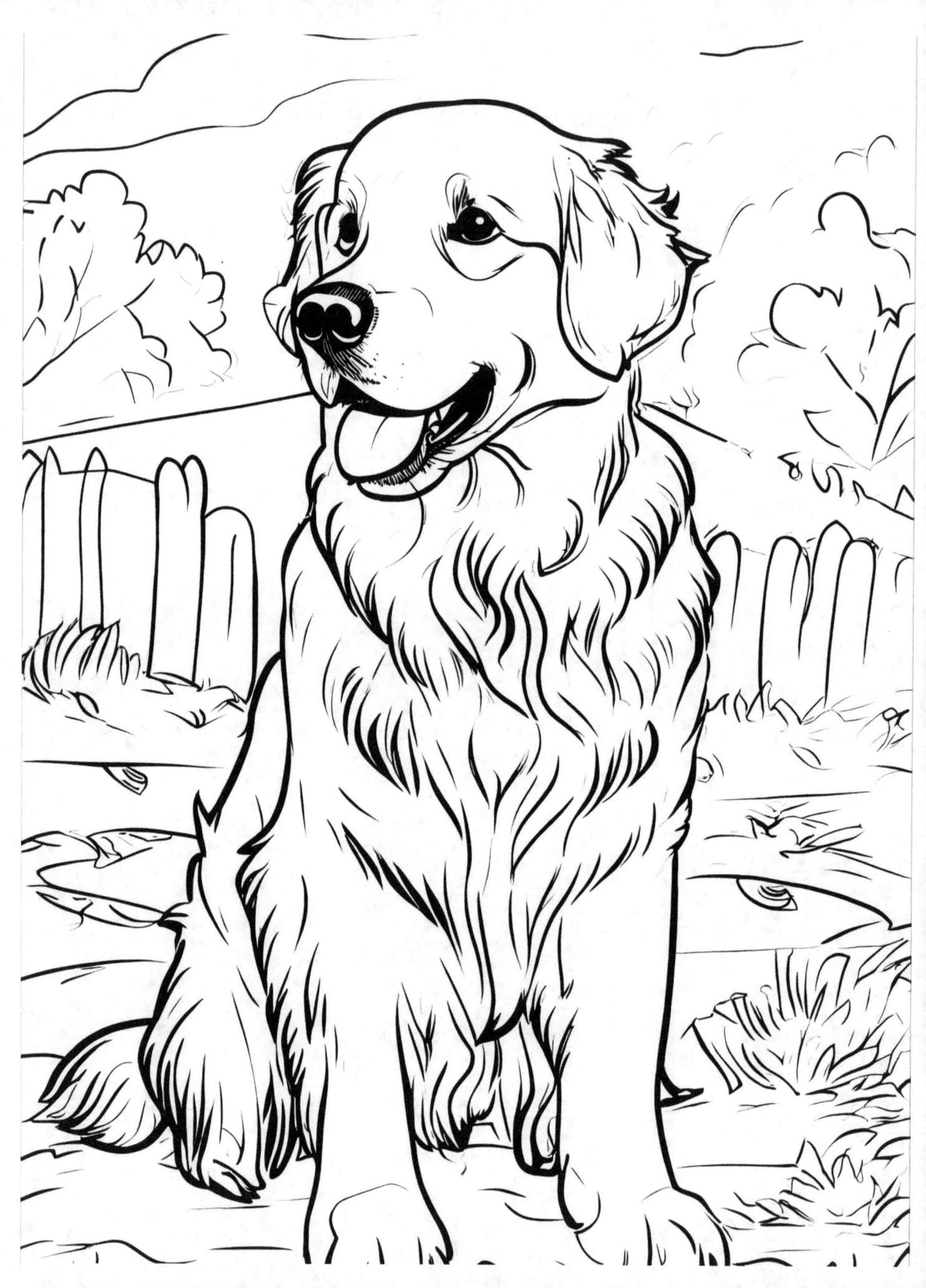

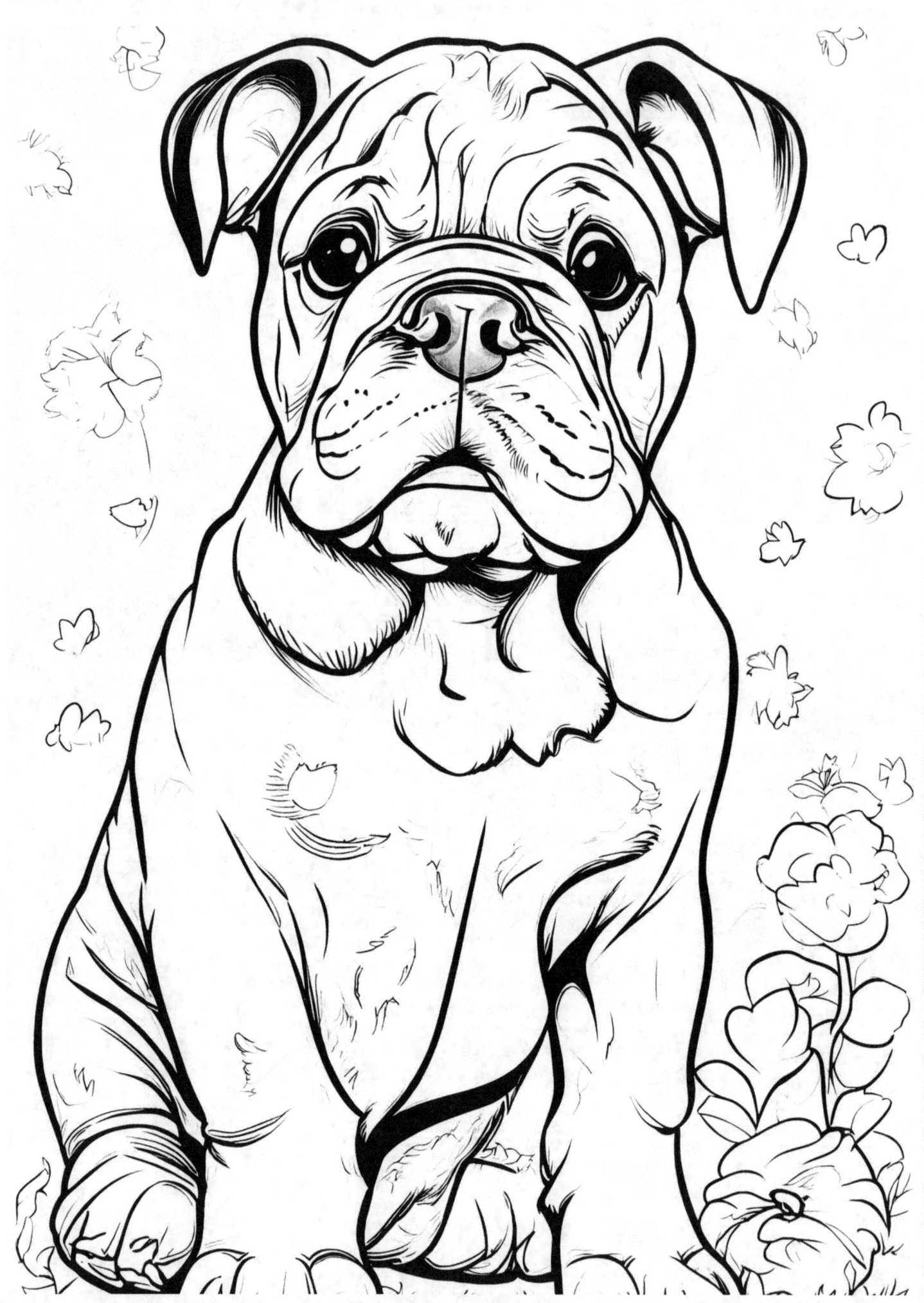

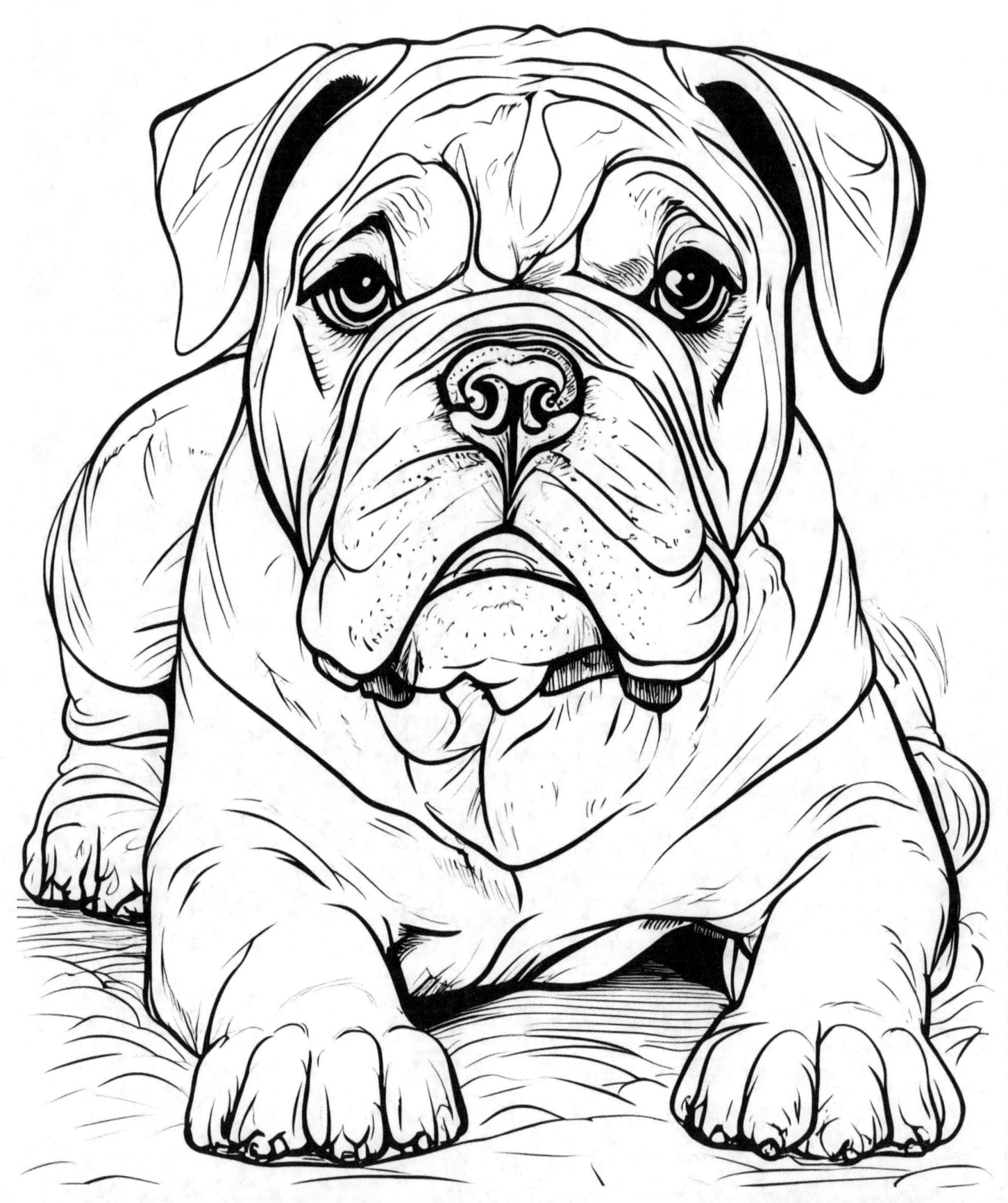

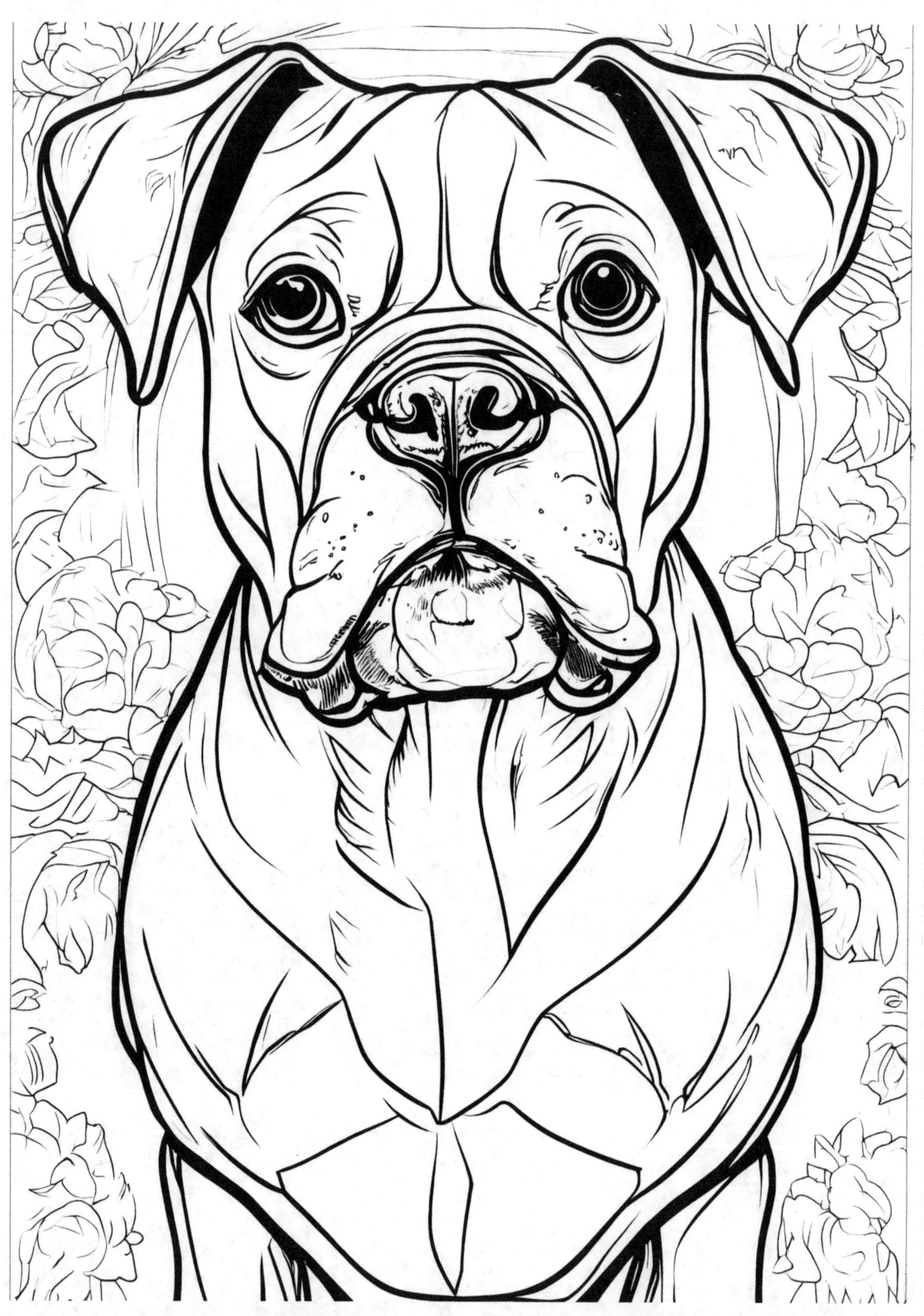

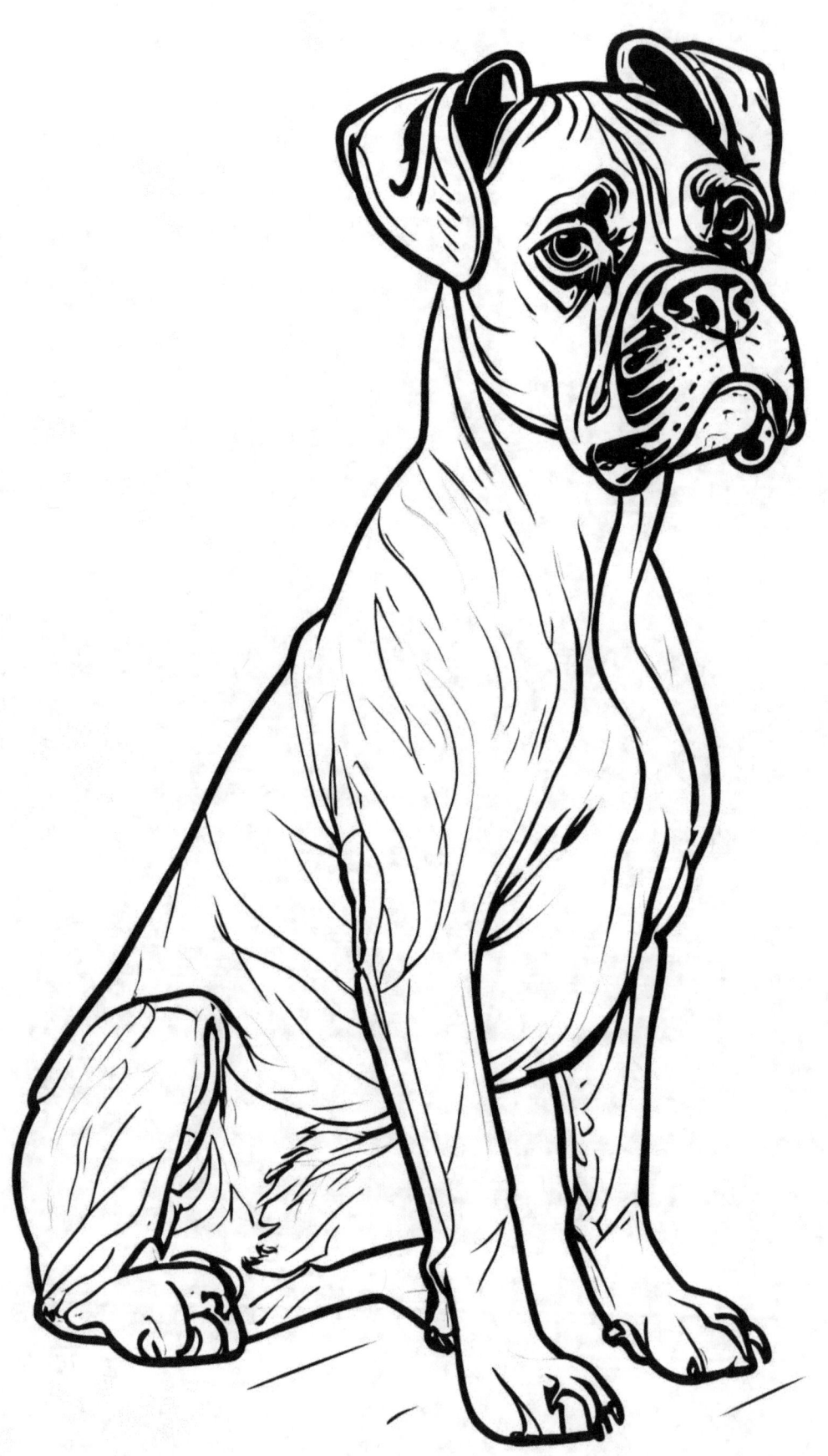

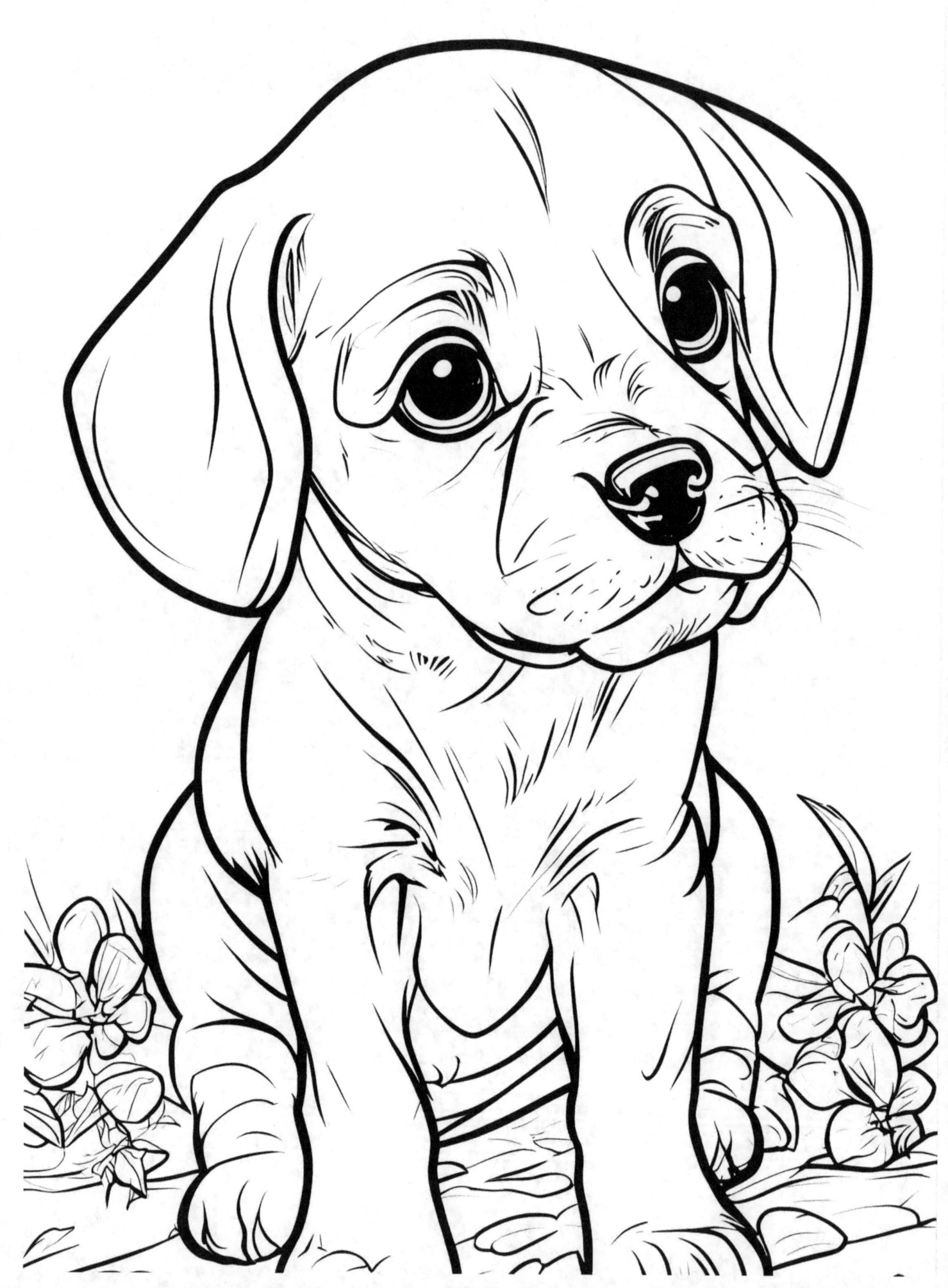

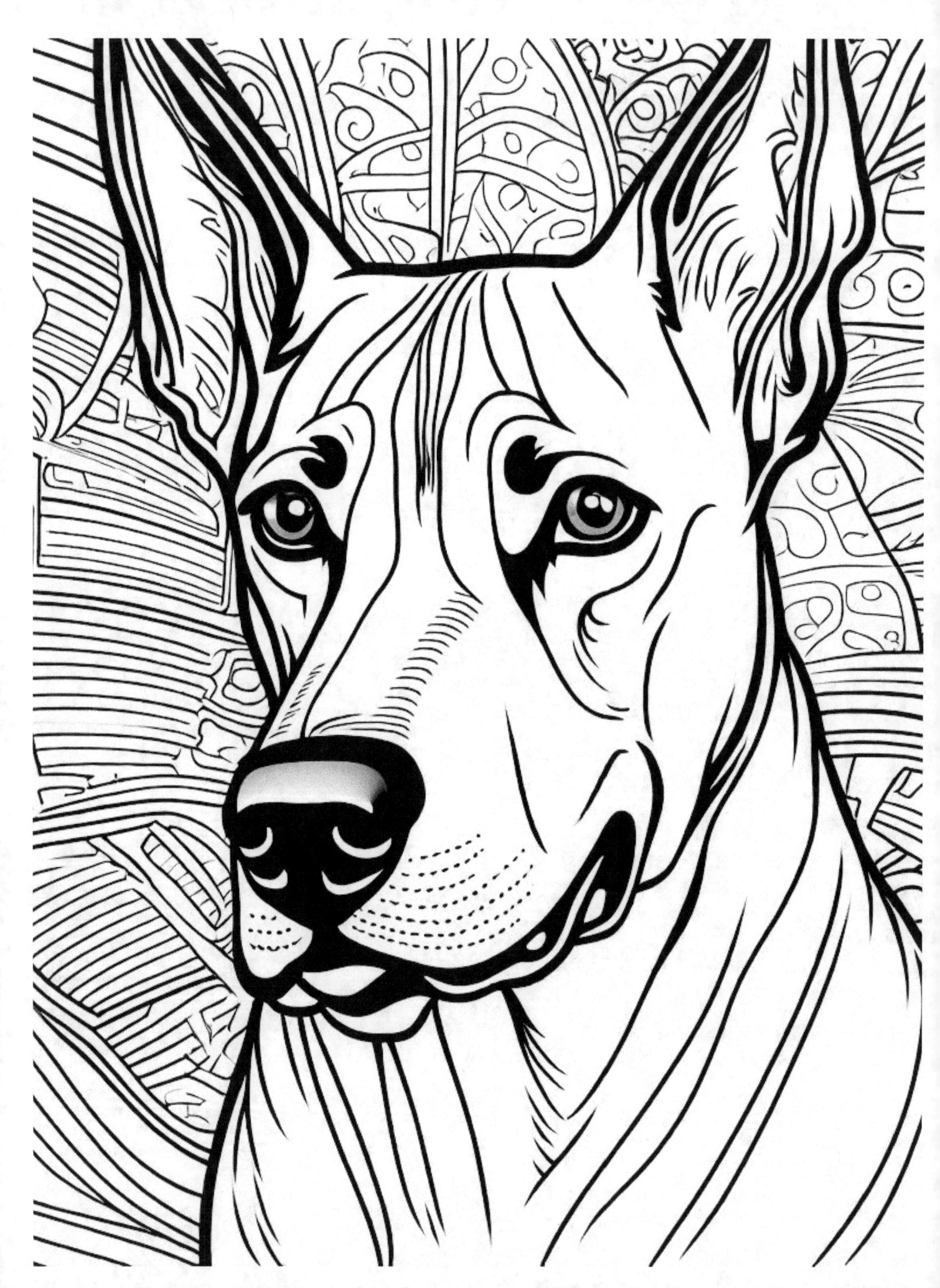

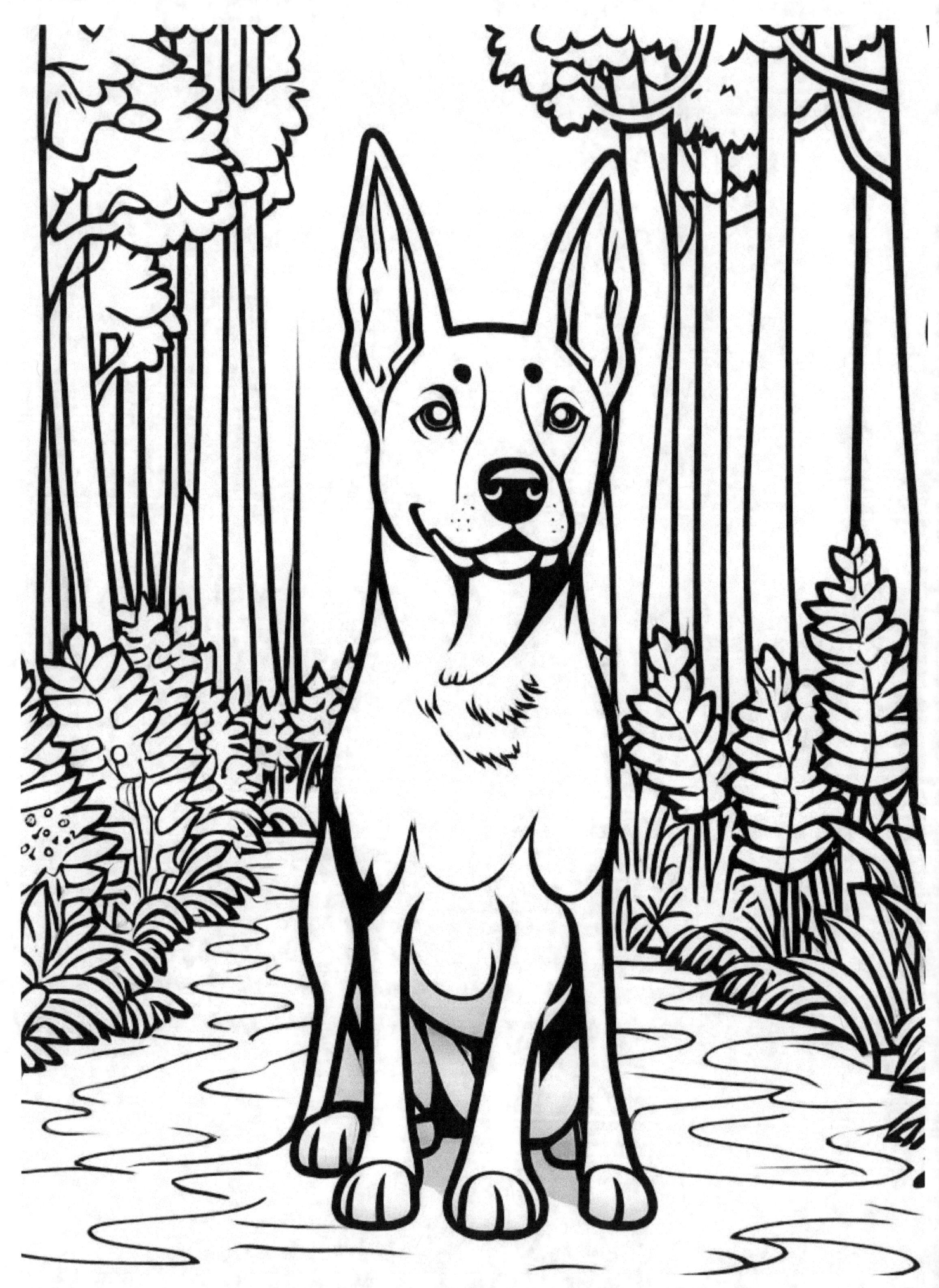

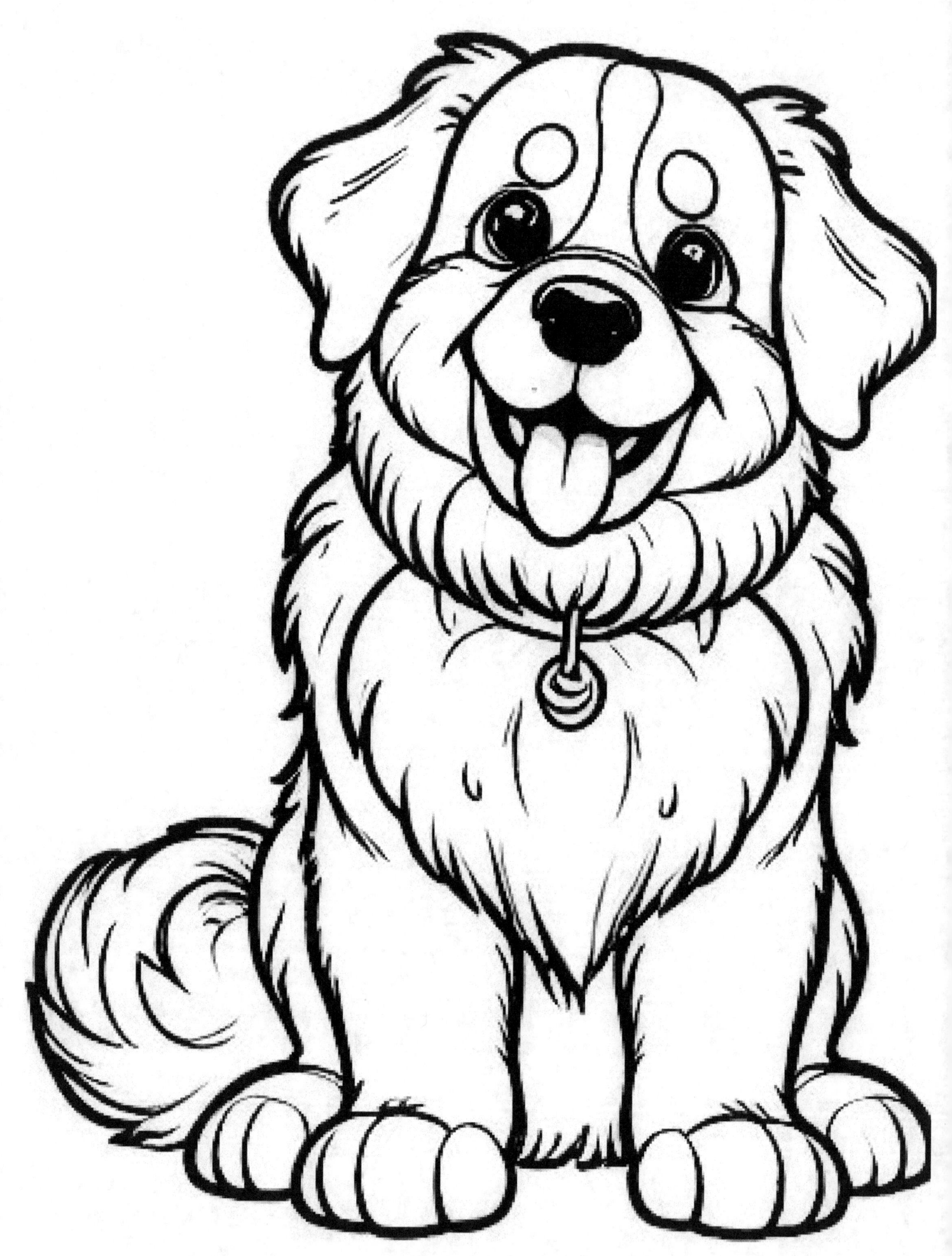

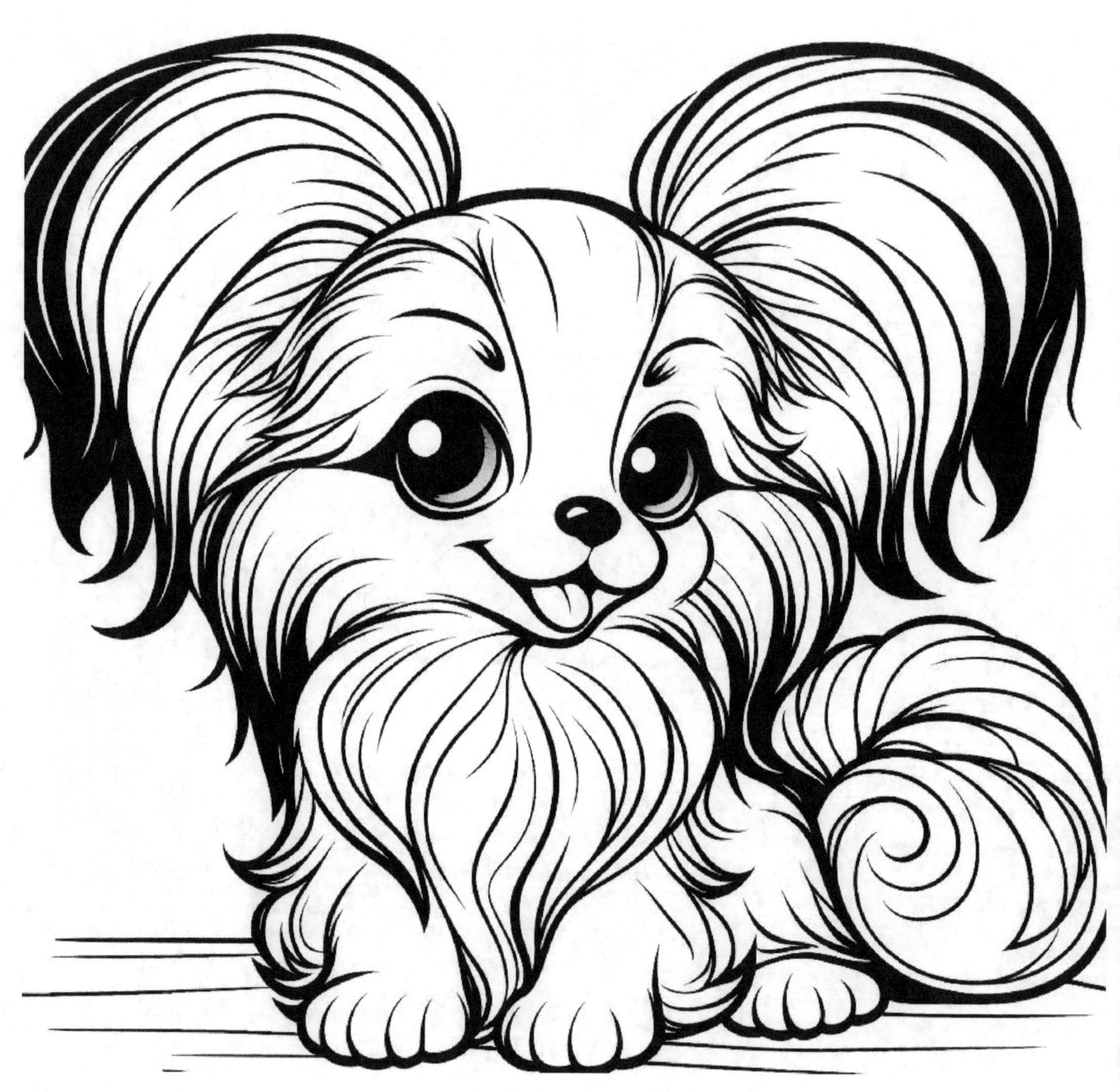

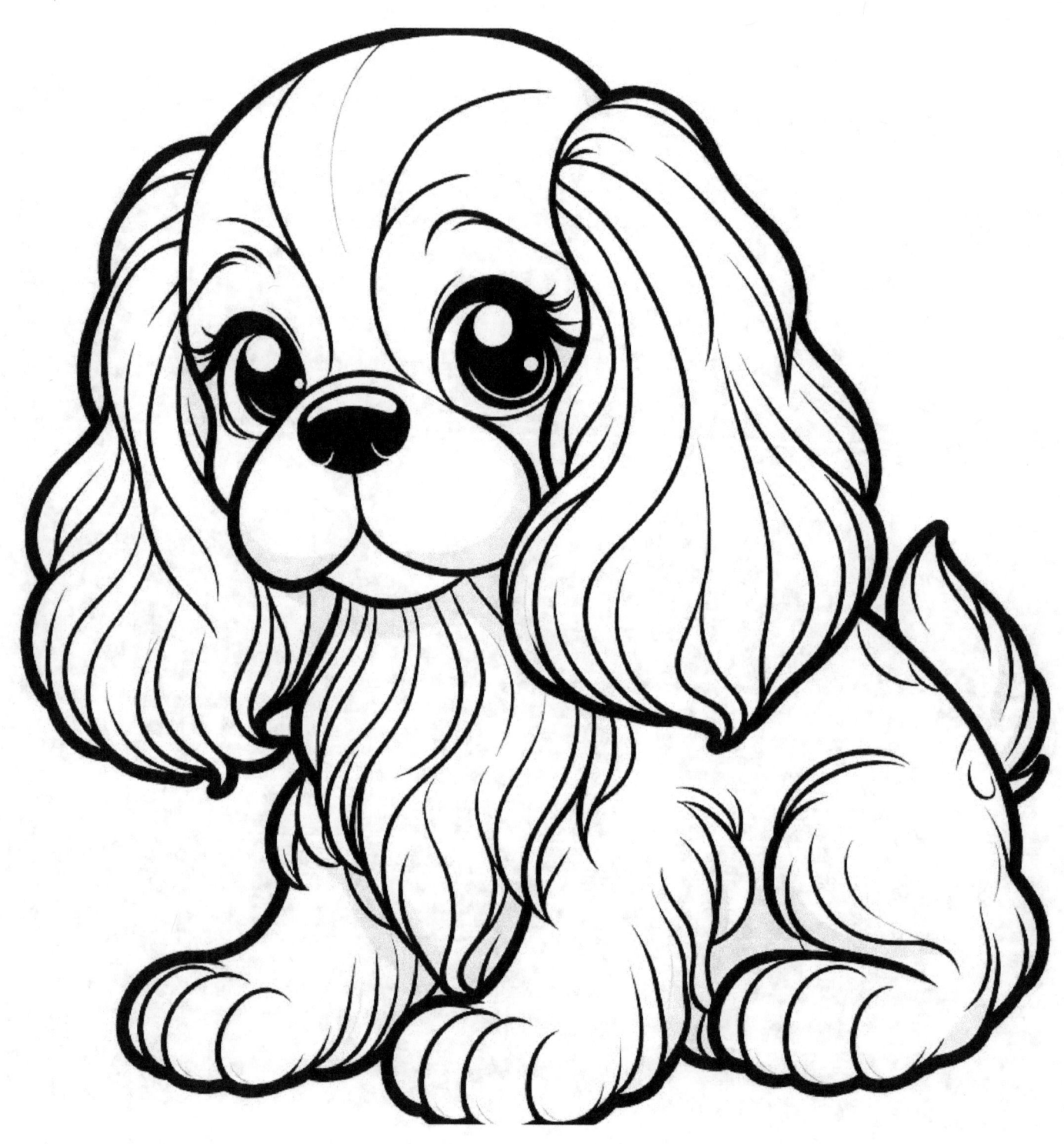

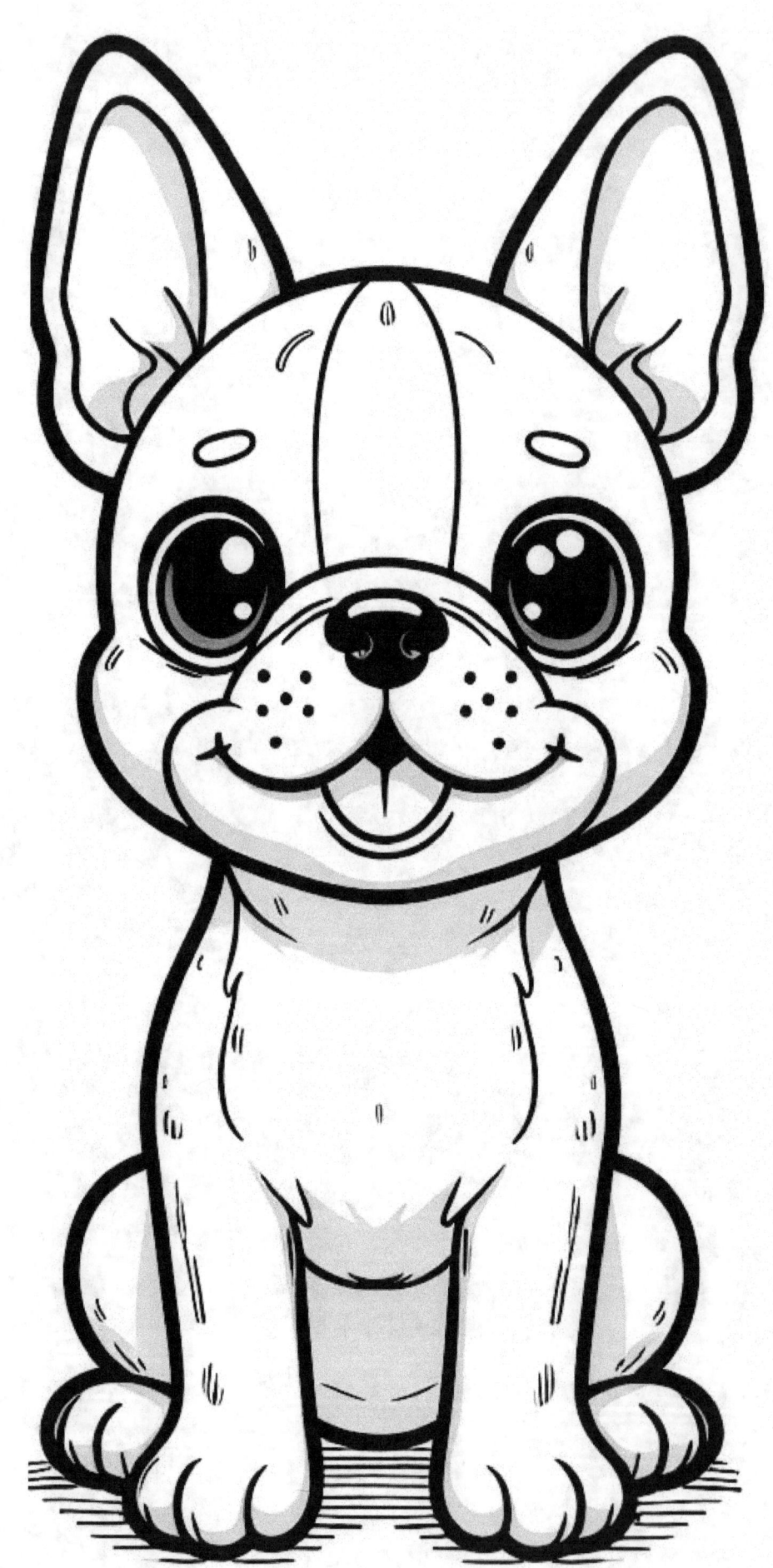

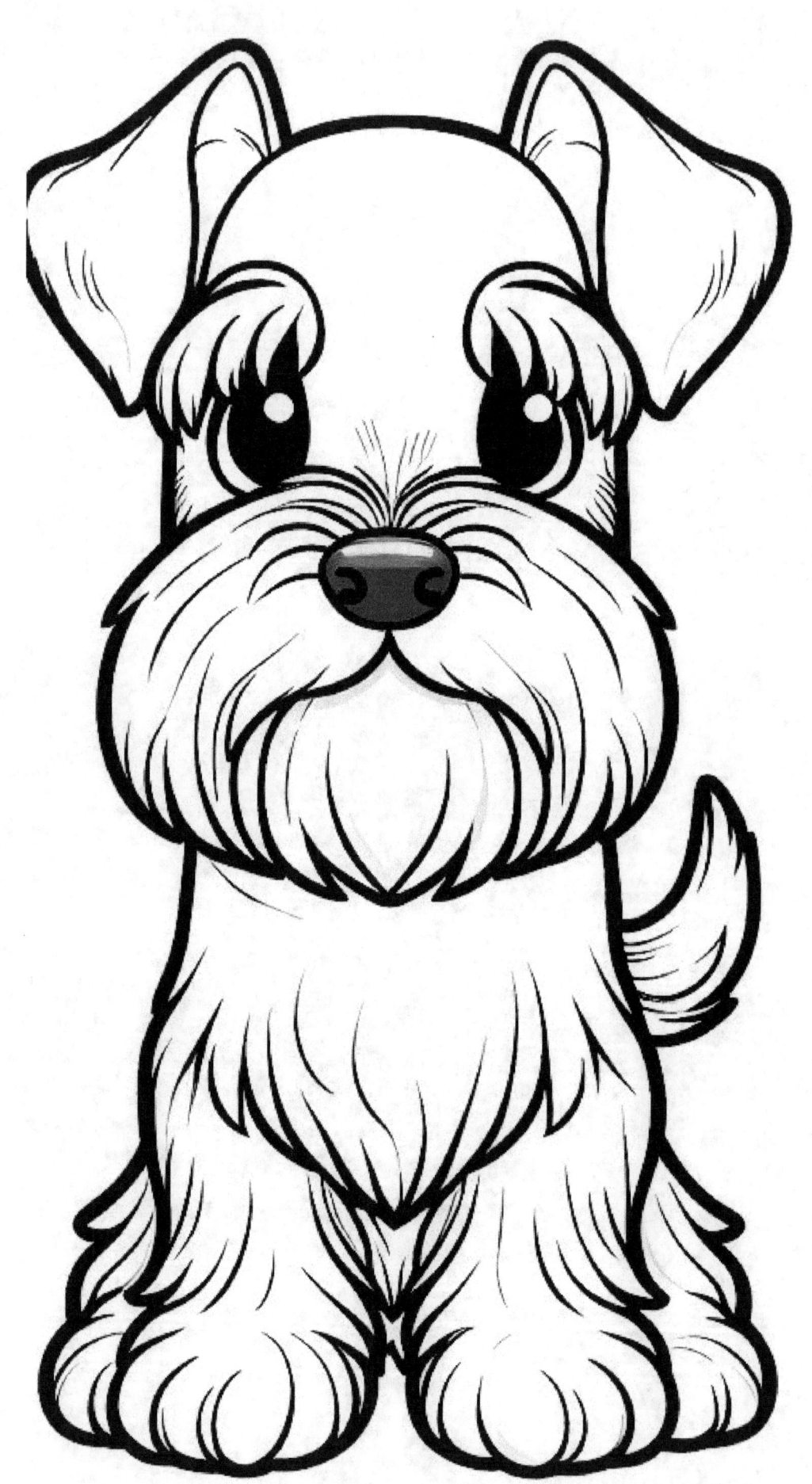

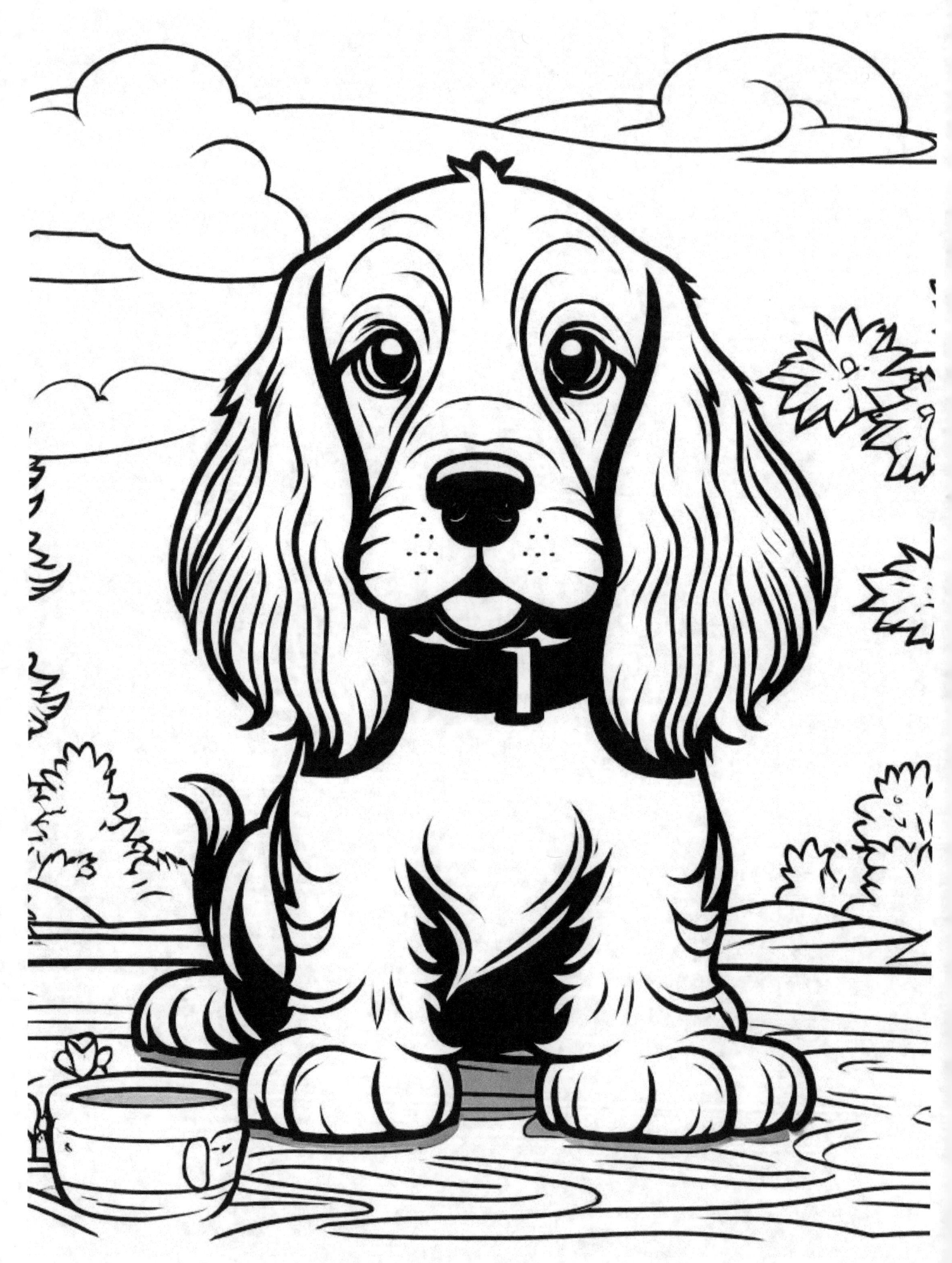

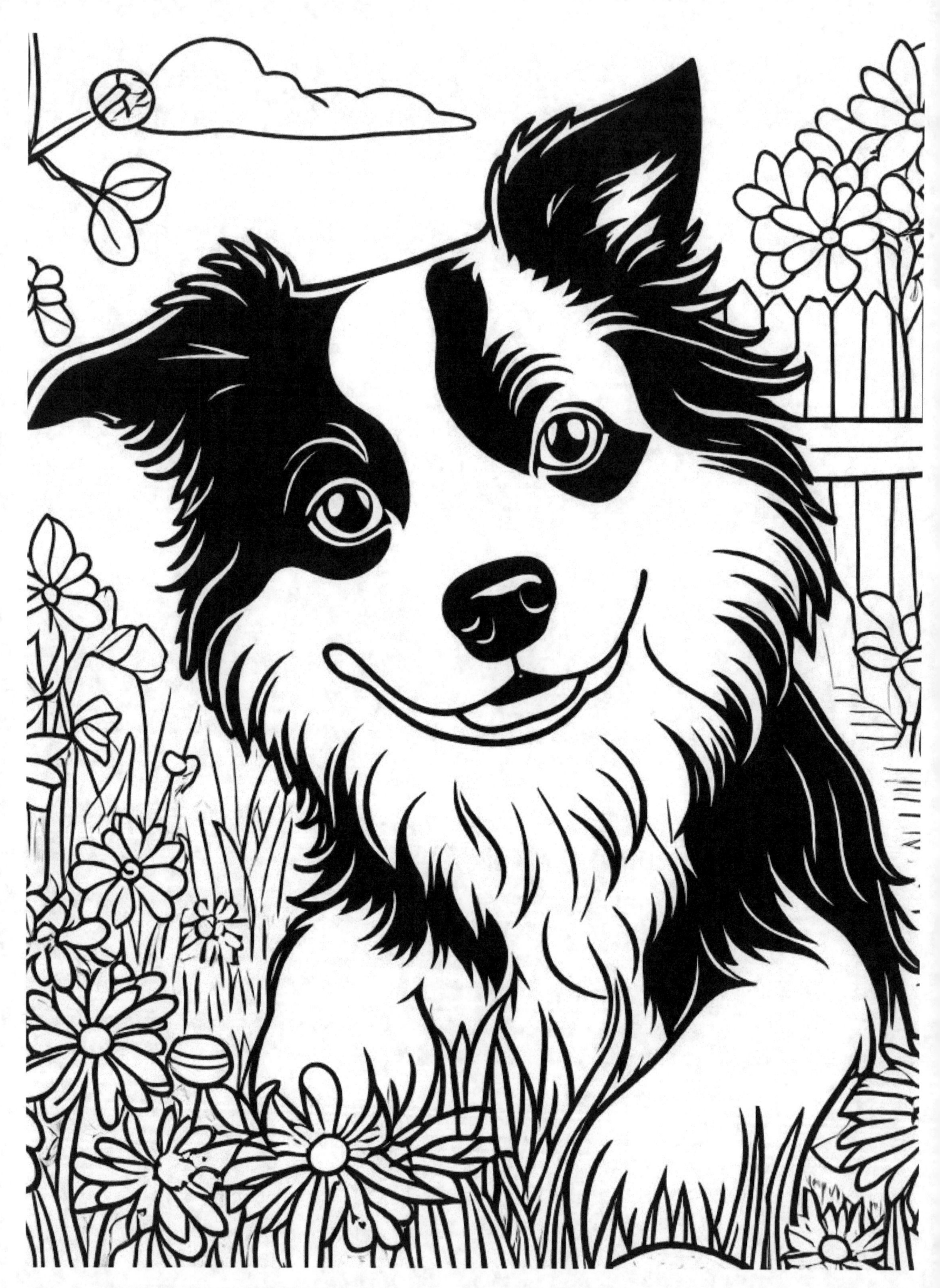

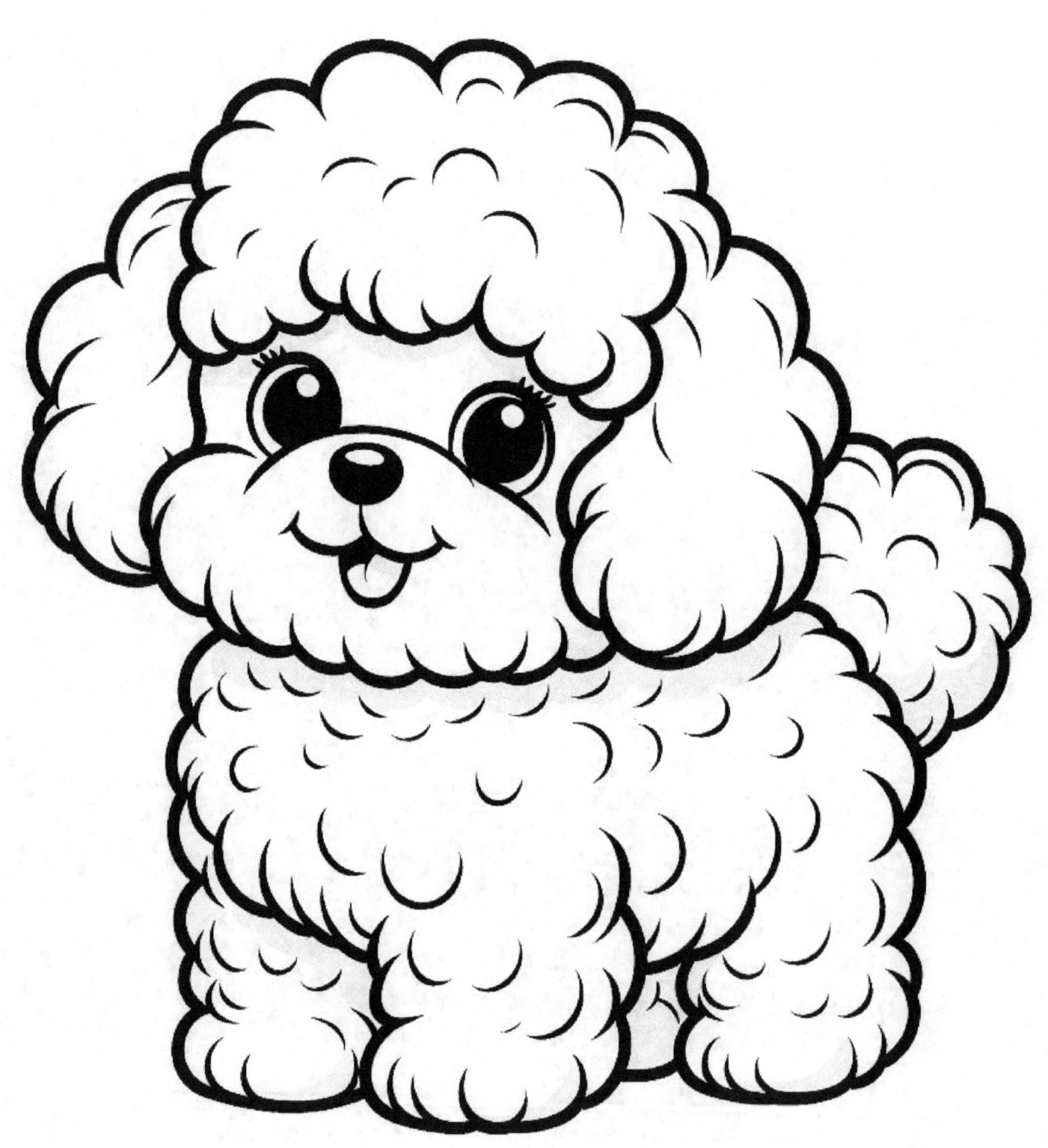

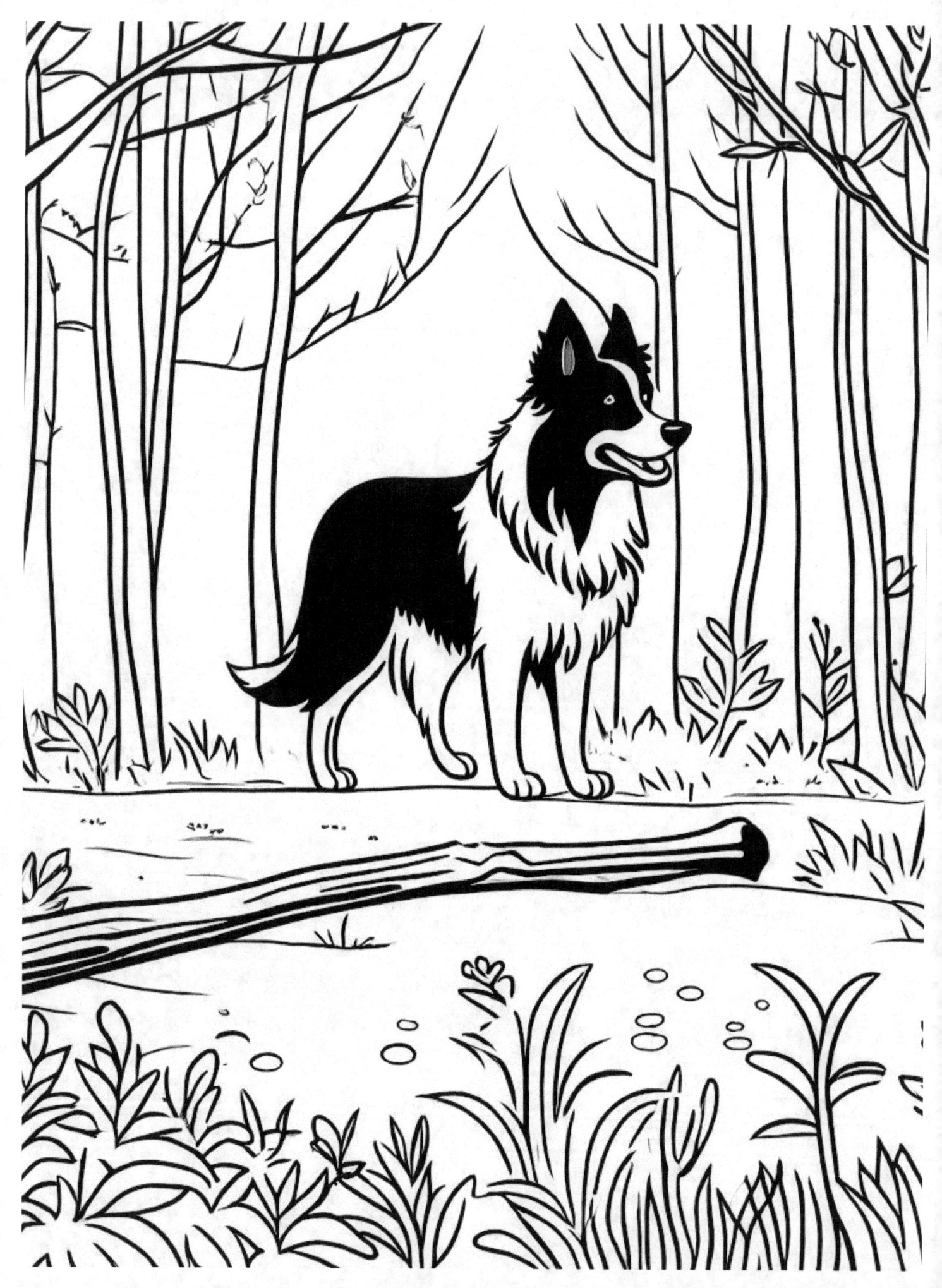

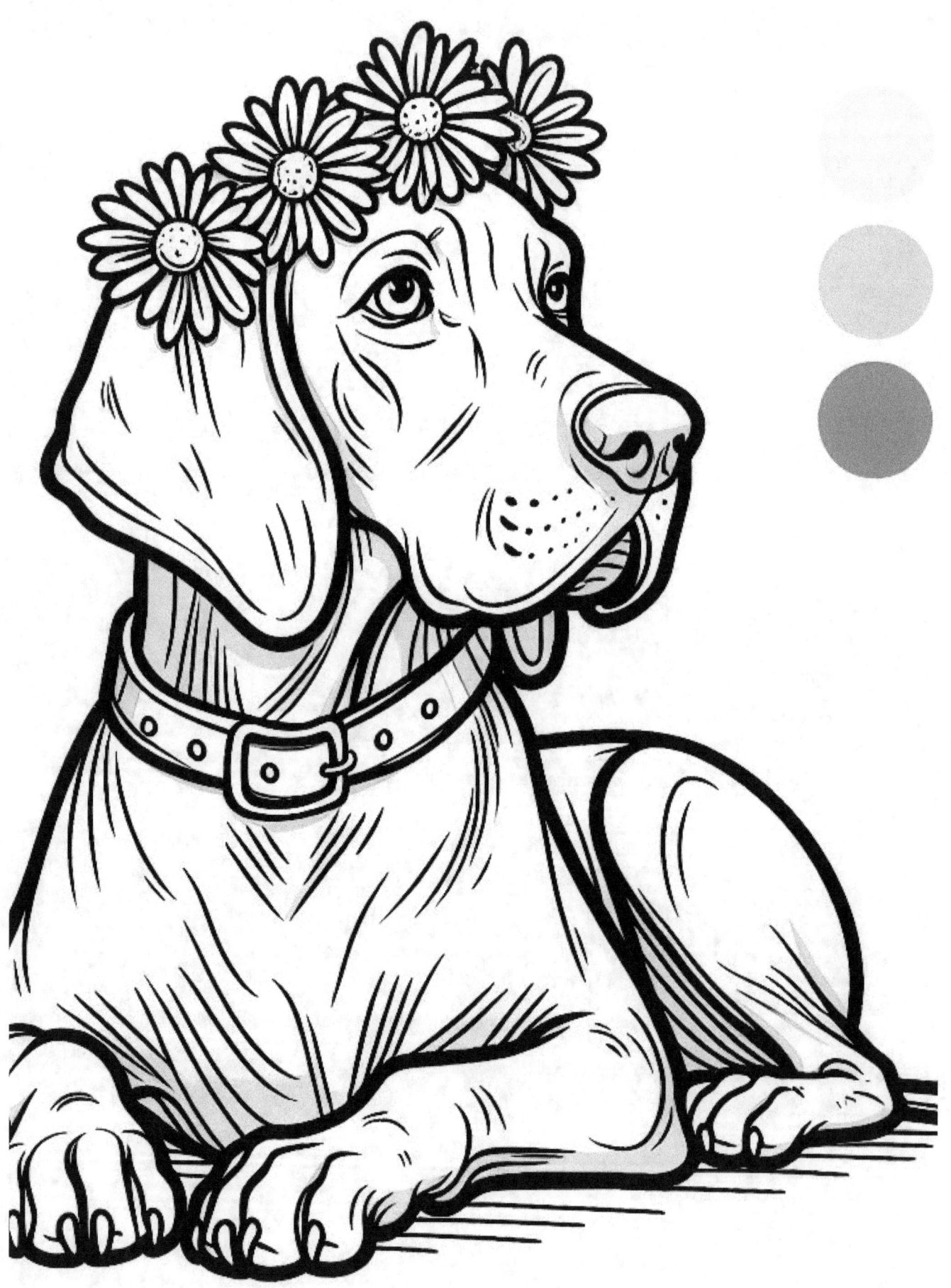

www.ingramcontent.com/pod-product-compliance
Lightning Source LLC
Chambersburg PA
CBHW062124220526
45471CB00010B/3863